The Kalergi Plan

The Kalergi plan can be found in the writings of psychotic eugenicist Richard von Coudenhove - Kalergi.

Kalergi was born on the 16th of November 1894. He was the son of Heinrich von Coudenhove – Kalergi, an Austro-Hungarian diplomat, and Mitsuko Aoyama, a Japanese woman. They met when Heinrich was in Japan representing his country. Mitsuko was the daughter of a Japanese oil merchant.

When Richard was eighteen years old, he met and married Ida Roland, a Jewish Austrian and German actress, who was thirteen years Richards` senior. Ida had never given Richard any children, but she had a daughter from a previous marriage.

Although the Kalergi plan was mapped out by Richard Kalergi, the idea was originally conceived by Austrian Baron Louis Nathaniel de Rothschild. The Rothschild family were the richest family in Europe and today are the richest family in the world. Their corruption runs so deep and goes back many centuries. I will go into more detail about the powerful

Rothschild family in another chapter.

In 1922, Richard Kalergi published his proposal called Pan-Europa. The Pan-Europa movement in Vienna aimed to create a one world government. Because of his father's association with European aristocrats, Richard had friends and associates in high places. One of the many influential people

Richard knew was Louis Nathaniel de Rothschild. It was de Rothschild who introduced Richard to the Warburgs, a powerful family who were in the business of banking with the Rothschild family. Max Warburg offered Richard the equivalent of 300,000 euros in todays` money. This money was to be used over a three-year period, to build a movement in Germany and elsewhere in Europe.

With this money he set up a publishing company for Pan-Europa. He then sold 40,000 copies of his proposal which helped him gain more influential and powerful supporters such as Austrian Chancellor Ignaz Seipal, Engelbert Dollfuss and Kurt

Schuschinigg, to name a few.

In 1925, Richard went on to publish another book titled, Pracktischer Idealismus (Practical Idealism). In this book he describes how our individual ethnicities will be diluted to create a new breed of mongrels who are easy to control, and all nations and borders will disappear to make a new European superstate. Kalergi wrote: *"The man of the future will be of mixed race. Todays` races and classes will disappear owing to the vanishing of space, time and prejudice. The Eurasian-Negroid race of the future, similar it its` appearance to the ancient Egyptians, will replace the diversity of peoples` with a diversity of individuals. Instead of destroying European Judaism, Europe, against her will, will be*

*refined through this
artificial evolutionary
process"*.

He promoted the idea
of abolishing nations
and he also promoted
mass immigration.
Europe's new mixed
race of people will have
no identity, nationalism
or traditions, and can
now be easily
controlled by his chosen
elites which would be
Jewish people.

In the 1950`s, James Warburg made horrendous globalist comments which attracted major attention. He stated, *"We shall have a world government, whether we like it or not. The question is whether it will be achieved by consent or by conquest"*. Conquest seems more likely because the majority of people would not consent to this plan. G.

Brock Chisholm, former director of the World Health Organization once said, *"What people in all places have to do is limit the birthrate in all places and promote mixed marriages as this aims to create a single race, in a world directed by one authority"*.

Because Kalergi thought Jewish people were superior and should rule the masses, many Jewish intellectuals had been massive supporters of the Pan-European movement. These include Albert Einstein, Bronislaw Huberman, Stefan Zweig, Sigmund Freud, Arthur Schnitzler, Bruno Kreisky, Franz Werfel and Andre Leon Blum.

The Pan-European Union was banned in Nazi Germany. Hitler despised Kalergi and his movement. He would often call him a "bastard" and belittled him calling him an "elitist half breed". In 1933, Kalergi visited Mussolini in Rome to try to get his support. He wanted a strong leader who would be in contact with the elites. Kalergi refused to condemn Mussolini`s invasion of Ethiopia as he thought that doing so would send Mussolini right into Hitlers arms. When

Austrian Chancellor, Schuschnigg, resigned, he was replaced by Arthur Seyss-Inquart, who was a Nazi sympathizer, he allowed German troops into the country. At this point, Kalergi and his wife, Ida, fled the country and immigrated to New York and there founded the Research Seminar for a Federative Postwar Europe at New York University. He tried to gain the support of President Roosevelt but failed to make an impression. Roosevelt thought of Kalergi as a nuisance. It was thanks to Winston Churchill and the Jewish B`nai B`rith freemasons that the Kalergi plan was eventually approved by the US government and eventually by the CIA also.

Kalergis` ideas form the basis of the

European Union. The
EU is a sort of prototype
of the Kalergi plan. He is
behind the EU ideal and
Europe Day. He chose
the EU anthem, and he
also influenced the
design of the EU flag.
There is even a postage
stamp in Austria
commemorating him.
Every year, the EU
bestow a prize to
people who have acted
in some way to
promote the Kalergi
plan. It is also known as

the Charlemagne prize
and recent winners are
Angela Merkel, Herman
van Rompuy, Tony Blair
and Henry Kissinger.
Why they won this
prize, we`ll never know
for sure. We can only
guess, but given their
history, their activities
are no doubt nefarious.

If you look around at
the world today, you
will see the Kalergi plan
being implemented. It
has accelerated

significantly since the covid "pandemic". Ethnic minorities are prioritized over Caucasians in the EU. Even though 60% of people coming into Europe are from Africa and the Middle East, using asylum seeker status as a cover, to question this in any way means you are a racist, according to the EU. One cannot question that the US government are paying for the

transport of migrants
into Europe, or that
French and Turkish
officials were caught
red handed selling
lifeboats to refugees in
Turkey, or that George
Soros insisted that the
EU spend 10billion
euros every year to
facilitate the movement
of a million Muslim
refugees into Europe.

All of this is to blend
Africans and Asians with
Europeans to breed a

new race of people.
There is proof of this by
professor Kamao
Kambon in 2005 when
he advocated for the
end of the white race.
David Cameron has also
said "too many white
Christian face in
Britain".

Former President of
the Czech Republic was
the first head of a
nation to accuse the EU
of working towards the
Kalergi plan. He stated,

"Migration is the method with which to dilute the current European countries to create a sort of docile people that will become the future Europeans. The dictators of the past, Hitler and Stalin have always wanted this, and the European elites are committing the same evils as those dictators".

It has occurred to me that the illegal attacks by the American - Isreali elite on Muslim countries such as Iraq, Afghanistan and Libya, have conveniently radicalised Muslim men and women who are now intent on revenge by war/invasion. Of course, the Muslim people are not at fault here. They have been played, just as much as we Europeans have. The fault lies with the elite and Europhiles, who are hell-bent on destroying Europe as laid out in the Kalergi plan.

The Rockefeller Foundation

John D. Rockefeller created the family-run Rockefeller Foundation in 1909. By 1929 he had put $300 million into the Standard Oil Company of New Jersey, which is now called Exxon. The money made from the oil company was used

to create Psychiatric
Genetics. He then
created and directed
the Kaiser Wilhelm
Institute for psychiatry
and the Kaiser Wilhelm
Institute for
Anthropology, Eugenics
and Human Heredity in
Germany. The chief
executive of these
institutes was Swiss
psychiatrist by the
name of Ernst Rudin. He
had two proteges who
worked with him,

Otmar Verschuer and Franz J. Kallmann.

In 1932, Rudin became the president of the British-led eugenics movement known as the worldwide eugenics' federation. This federation called for the killing or sterilization of people whose heredity made them a burden to society. This eugenics idea would go on to become a section of the Nazi state. The Nazi`s appointed Rudin the head of the Racial Hygiene Society. Rudin and his proteges were a part of a task force consisting of heredity experts, chaired by Heinrich Himmler.

The German chemical company I.G. Farben was led by the Warburg family who were the Rockefellers' partners in banking and in eugenics. In 1940, I.G. Farben built a factory at

Auschwitz
concentration camp.
They used the Jewish
prisoners as slave labor
to work in the factory to
make gas from coal. SS
guards were assigned to
select prisoners to work
at the factory and those
who were unfit were
sent off to be killed. I
must mention that one
of Farbens` subsidiaries
supplied the gas, Zyklon
B, which would kill
millions of people in the
gas chambers.

In 1936, Rockefellers`
doctor, Franz Kallmann
emigrated to the US
because he was half
Jewish. He ended up in
New York and while
there he founded the
medical genetics
department of the New
York State Psychiatric
Institute. Kallmann then
wrote a report on the
study of schizophrenia,
and it was published by
the Scottish Rite of
Freemasonry. It was
this book which was

used by the Nazis to rationalize the murder of mental patients and "defective" people. 250,000 people were killed under this program.

Verschuer, another one of Rockefellers doctors, secured funds from the Rockefellers for his new assistant, the infamous, Josef Mengele. With these funds, Mengele would go on to perform horrific experiments at Auschwitz. Especially on twins as they were his favorite to experiment on. He would get the twins to fill out an extremely detailed form for the Rockefellers Kaiser Wilhelm Institute. All prisoners at Auschwitz would have daily drawings of blood, needles were inserted into eyes to study eye color, experimental blood transfusions were performed which often led to infection, organs and limbs were removed, sometimes without anesthetics, sex changes were attempted, females were sterilized, and males were castrated. After prisoners had their organs, eyeballs, heads, and limbs removed, the body were then sent to Verschuer and the Rockefellers at the Kaiser Wilhelm Institute to be studied. The atrocities committed at Auschwitz were funded, for the most part, by the Rockefeller Foundation. After the war, the Rockefellers helped to set up a sub-committee of the eugenics society called the International Planned Parenthood Federation.

By the start of the 20th century, John D. Rockefeller became the first billionaire in the

US, having 90% control over oil refineries. In 1900 his researchers discovered it was possible to make chemicals from oil and so the first plastic, bakelite, was made from oil. His researchers then realized that vitamins could also be produced from oil. Monopolizing the chemical and medical industries, as well as the oil business was extremely financially

rewarding for
Rockefeller. At that
time, petrochemicals
were a new discovery
and could be patented
but the only thing
getting in the way was
the popularity of
natural remedies in the
US at the time. He
needed to get rid of the
competition. This led to
the Flexner Report. In
this report, it was
stated that medical
institutions need to be
revamped. This led to

natural remedies and
homeopathy were
rubbished and those
who still practiced
holistic medicine were
sent to prison.
Rockefeller then gave
over $100 million to
medical facilities and
colleges to change the
minds of doctors and
researchers. This is a
system which focuses
on the symptoms and
not the root of the
problem, as this
produces a constant

supply of patients and their money.

John D. Rockefeller poured a significant amount of money into the American education system. He created the General Education Board which cost $129 million. His motives for this were well known as he once stated, *"I don`t want a nation of thinkers, I want a nation of workers"*. Frederick T. Gates, a member of the General Education board stated, "*We shall try not to make these children into philosophers or men of learning, or men of science*".

Money and power corrupt, and when one has too much of both, they tend to not let things like ethics or basic human decency get in their way.

The Rothschild Family

Behind the scenes, the Rothschild family are the most powerful family on Earth. They own the world's financial system, and their wealth is estimated to be over $500 trillion. The bank of international settlement, which was established in 1931, is fully owned by the Rothschild family. This bank is considered the top bank and every central bank is a member.

There are two banks which offer loans to all countries on the planet. These are the World bank and the IMF. The world bank is owned by some of the world's top banking families with, of course, the Rothschilds being the main shareholder. The IMF though, is privately

owned by the
Rothschilds alone.
These two banks offer
loans to poorer
countries with interest
rates that are near
impossible to pay back.
The family has so much
wealth that they are
able to bribe politicians
to steer policy decisions
in whatever direction
they chose. They have
funded both sides of
every war since the
Napoleanic wars
because they financially

benefit from it. They care nothing for the millions of lives lost, if they continue to accumulate more wealth. Human life means nothing to them.

In 1815, after Nathan Mayer Rothschild bought and paid for England, he made the following statement: *"I care not what puppet is placed on the throne of England to rule the Empire on which the sun never sets. The man who controls Britain's money supply controls the British Empire, and I control the British money supply"*.

The Rothschilds agenda for depopulation has been centuries in the making. In 1928, British writer, H.G. Wells, laid out the RothschildsKalergi plan for depopulation in his book `The Open Conspiracy Plans for World Revolution`. In this is a step-by-step plan the Rothschilds and their agents have followed. The Rothschilds, by the way, commissioned this book. I have no idea why they would want their plans known to world. To put into perspective how close they are to total world domination, here is a passage from H.G. wells` book, *"A one world government and a one world monetary system under hereditary oligarchs. In this one world, population will be limited by restriction on the number of children per family, disease, war, and famines until one billion people, who are useful to the ruling class, remain. There will be no middle class, only rulers and servants. Only one religion will be allowed and that will be in the form of a one world government church, which has been in existence since 1920. To induce a state where there is no individual freedom or any concept of liberty surviving, there shall be no such thing as republicanism, sovereignty, or rights residing with the people. National pride and racial identity shall be stamped out. At least four billion useless eaters shall be eliminated by the year 2050 by means of limited wars, organized epidemics, and rapid-acting diseases and starvation. No city shall be larger than a predetermined number as described in the works of Kalergi. From time to time there shall be artificially contrived food and water shortages and medical care to remind the masses that their very existence depends on the goodwill of the elites".*

A century later one need only look at the world to see this plan coming to fruition. We are facing crypto-currencies, vaccine passports, social credit scores, track and trace, pandemics, sustainable smart cities, forced vaccination, racial wars, social unrest, the eradication of automobiles, forced dependency on the state, the culling of the weak and the elderly,

Rothschild funded nonprofit organizations flooding majority white countries with refugees whilst instigating hatred against white Christians, a society where human life has no value and morals are in short supply. The Rothschilds have infiltrated governments, companies, and royal families around the world through debt and/or interbreeding. It is they who pull the

strings and are
responsible for the
terrifying direction
society is going in. They
benefit financially from
chaos.

Klaus Schwab and the World Economic Forum

Klaus Schwab was born in 1938 in Nazi Germany. His father, Eugen Schwab was the managing director of the Swiss company, Escher-Wyss AG. This company was responsible for the production of machinery which was critical for the Nazi war effort as well as producing heavy water for the Nazis nuclear program. While Eugen Schwab was chief executive, the company was awarded the title `National Socialist Model Company`, possibly because it used slave labor. The company had set up camps for the "workers" on the premises.

Years later, when Klaus served on the board of directors, the company had made the decision to play a role in the development of South Africa's` nuclear weapons program. The company helped the regime in South Africa to build six nuclear weapons. It`s worth mentioning that while Klaus attended Harvard, he was taught by the war criminal, Henry Kissinger.

Schwab founded the World Economic Forum in 1971 when he was 32 years old. It was originally called the European Management Forum up until 1987. Initially, the forum only gathered people from the economic field together, but soon, it attracted many prominent figures from the media, politicians, and even celebrities. I have no doubt that this was because of his friendship with Henry Kissinger.

Schwab established another institution in 1992 called The Global Leaders for Tomorrow. The name was changed in 2004 to Young Global Leaders. The people attending this school had to first apply for admission before being subjected to a rigorous selection process. There are 1,300 graduates from this school, a lot of them are politicians, but it is not limited to just politicians. On the schools` alumni list, names such as Bill Gates, Jeff Bezos, Richard Branson, Jimmy Wales (Wikipedia founder), and Chelsea Clinton were found there.

The World Economic
Forum has groomed
several people who
then infiltrated
governments around
the world. Schwab, in
2014, called for the
Great Reset. A social
construct to assign
every human with an
electronic ID which
would be linked to our
bank accounts, health
records, and online
activity and behaviors.
The global elite would
then have the power to

constantly monitor and control people. This is already happened in China.

In June 2019, an agreement was signed between the World Economic Forum and the United Nations which promises to accelerate the "implementation of Agenda 2030 for sustainable development". Gonzalo Berrón of the Transnational Institute said, *"This agreement between the UN and the WEF formalizes a disturbing corporate capture of the UN. It moves towards a privatized and undemocratic global governance"*. Schwab wrote his book "The 4th industrial revolution in 2018, and it is, without a doubt, terrifying to say the least. In this book, he wrote, *"We will become better able to manipulate our own genes, and those of our children. Where do we draw the line between human and machine? What does it mean to be human?"*. Does this man not know what it means to be human?

At the January 2020 WEF meeting, futurist-historian, and Schwab's `right hand man`, Yuval Noah Harari stated, *"We hear about the enormous promises of technology, but technology might*

*disrupt human society
and the very meaning of
being human in
numerous ways,
ranging from the global
useless class to the rise
of colonialism and of
digital dictatorships.
Soon, some
governments and
corporations will be
able to hack all people.
We humans should get
used to the idea that we
are no longer
mysterious souls – we
are now hackable*

animals". This is frightening because we're well on the way to this in the form of vaccine passes and digital ID. Another horrifying quote of his, which I lose sleep thinking about, is as follows, *"Humans and machines might merge so completely that humans might not be able to survive at all if they are disconnected from the network. They will be connected starting in the womb, and later in life, if they chose to disconnect, insurance companies might refuse to insure you, employers might refuse to employ you, and healthcare services might refuse to take care of you"*. I find his overuse of the word human extremely unsettling. He speaks about humans as if he isn`t one...

In February 2022, the World Economic Forum

released a report,
"Advancing Digital
Agency: The power of
data intermediaries". In
this report, it details
their plans to create the
4th industrial revolution.
It mentions the fusion
of the physical, digital,
and biological world. It
also states that the
covid "pandemic" has
led to a heightened
focus on the power of
medical data,
specifically the vaccine
passports. According to

the report, digital ID is glorified, and they shall include your profile which will have your name and national identity number, your history, which will have your medical history, credit history, online purchases and behavior. These self-appointed elites want our most private data, and they will do this by any means necessary. They plan to do this by implanting devices into our bodies, our homes, and our cities. The future will include constant surveillance of us and our surroundings through the internet of bodies (IOB) ecosystem. I know all this sounds like the rantings of a conspiracy lunatic to some close-minded people, but the proof is everywhere. It used to be hidden to us "useless eaters" but since the covid "pandemic" they aren`t trying to hide their plans anymore. They flaunt it in our faces. The RAND corporation in the USA says that IOB system is an ecosystem of a bunch of devices that are connected to the internet which contains software that collects our personal and health data. In time, these devices will be able to control our behavior too. The WEF global risk report in 2019 admitted, "authoritarianism is easier in a world of total visibility and traceability". The report also states, *"At their most basic level, they facilitate the exchange of information; at their most sophisticated, they can assume decision making on behalf of the people"*. Everything I have mentioned can be found online, in articles, and even on the World Economic Forums website itself. Many people will not believe the things that are happening right now because that would mean admitting to themselves that almost everything, they thought they knew was a lie. It`s hard for some people to admit this but I fully believe that when it comes to world events, there are no coincidences.

In 2016, the WEF published "8 predictions

of the world in 2030",
but these are their real
plans with the result
being total control.

1: All products will
become services. (You
will own nothing and be
happy)

2: A global price on
carbon

3: US dominance is
over, instead there will
be a handful of global
powers.

4: Farewell hospital.
The hospital as we

know it will be gone as there will be fewer road accidents because of self-driving cars, organ donors will be gone, and bio-printed organs will be a thing.

5: Less meat will be eaten.

6: Todays` refugees will be 2030`s CEO`s. Climate change will displace 1billion people.

7: The values of the West will be tested.

8: Ready to move humans to the red planet.

  People will borrow necessities from the state, goods will be rationed in line with a social credit score system, every move will be tracked electronically, clean energy requirements will be met, food will be mostly vegetarian, global agencies will set the price of CO_2

emissions at high levels to stop its use.

In 1972, The Club of Rome published a book titled, "The limits to growth". It focused on global overpopulation. The founder of the club of Rome was Aurelio Peccei and spoke at the third WEF annual meeting in 1973 summarizing the book. The same year, the club of Rome published a report detailing an adaptive model for global governance that would divide the world into ten states. They also published a controversial book in 1991 called "The first global revolution". In the book there is a passage which states, *"In searching for a common enemy against whom we can unite, we came up with the idea of pollution, global warming, water shortages, and famine"*.

What this tells me is that global warming is a hoax to make the masses live in fear. A fearful population is easier to control.

In 1993, MI-6 whistle-blower, Dr John Coleman published his book "Conspirator's Hierarchy: The story of the committee of 300. What was written in this book can be compared to the end goal which the WEF is striving for today. Coleman writes:

- The non-elite masses will be reduced to the level and behaviour of controlled animals with no will of their own and easily controlled.
- Marriage shall be outlawed and there shall be no family life as we know it.

- Children will be removed from their parents at an early age and brought up by wards as state property.
- One world government and one-unit monetary system, under non-elected, hereditary oligarchs.
- Population will be limited by restriction on the number of children

per family, famine, war, and disease.

- No middle class, just rulers and servants.
- All laws will be backed by one world police force and one world military.
- Rebellious people will be starved to death or declared outlaws.
- All Christian churches will be destroyed.

- No individual freedom.
- No republicanism or sovereignty.
- Racial identity will be destroyed.
- People will be given an identification number marked on their person. The numbers will be accessible through a master file in the NATO computer in Brussels.
- Self-abortion will be taught and will

be practised after
two children.

- If a woman gets
pregnant after
having two
children, she will be
forcibly removed to
an abortion clinic
for an abortion or
sterilization.
- Pornography will be
compulsory, shown
in every theatre.
- Drugs will be given
in food and water
without consent.

- People will be indoctrinated to understand that they are totally dependent on the state.
- All wealth will be in the hands of the committee of 300.
- Food production will be strictly controlled.
- Euthanasia will be compulsory for the terminally in and elderly.

- No city will be larger than what was described in the works of Kalergi.
- Breaking the law means instant execution.
- If you break the rules, your digital ID will be blacklisted, meaning no services.
- All media will be controlled by the

one world
government.
· Brainwashing
disguised as
entertainment.

One tool they are
using for mass
slavery is the
education system.
Schools teach
children to
memorize without
thinking and obey
without question.
The self-appointed
elites want our

children to learn
conformity and to
think inside the
box. They don't
want educated
people who are
capable of critical
thinking, they want
obedient robots
who are smart
enough to work the
machines but
stupid enough to
not ask questions.

Bill Gates

Bill Gates senior was
the co-founder of
Preston Gates and Ellis,
which was an
international law firm in
the US, China and
Taiwan. He was a
prominent lawyer who
was also involved in
politics and, of course,
philanthropy. Bill Sr sat
on the board of Margret
Sangers` planned
parenthood. The same

woman who once said, *"The most merciful thing a large family does to one of its infant members is to kill it".* Margret had a magazine named *"The birth control review",* and it received regular contributions from non-other than Ernst Rudin, who served as Hitler's director of genetic sterilization which I have mentioned in a previous chapter.

In 2000 Bill said it seems like every corner they turn; the Rockefellers were already there. Because they too fund controversial research, depopulation programs, behavior modification and the disgustingly twisted experiments of Pedophile Alfred Kinsey. I personally can't bring myself to write about Kinseys` experiments because they are horrifying and involve infant children all the way up to twelve years old.

Mary Gates, Bill Gates` mother, built a relationship with John Opel, the CEO of IBM. Opel had mentioned Gates to his fellow executives, and they decided to take a chance on Microsoft. But neither Bill, nor Microsoft co-founder, Paul Allen wrote the software code. It was not Bills` invention. The system Bill came up with was based on Gary Kildalls` work. Bill Gates tweaked it a little, renamed it and passed it off as his own.

Fast forward to 2010, at a TedTalk, Bill stated, *"The world today has 6.8billion people. Now that's leading up to 9billion. If we do a really great job on new vaccines, health care and reproductive health, we could lower that by perhaps 10 or 15%"*.

In 2000, Bill Gates started the Global Alliance for Vaccines and Immunization (GAVI) and he donated $750 million to the foundation. On the GAVI website, it boasts that is has helped to vaccinate more than 888 million children in the worlds` poorest countries. The World Health Organization has admitted that Bill Gates has given 496,000 Indian children polio through the polio vaccine. He is now wanted in India for crimes against humanity. I should mention that when Bill Gates wanted to administer the covid 19 vaccine on the Indian people, the Indian government wanted to launch their own independent investigation into the vaccine, but it was refused. This makes me wonder what they are hiding.

By 2018, 75% of the polio cases in India were from the polio vaccine. In 2014, Bill gave the HPV vaccine to 23,000 Indian girls. Many had severe side effects, seven girls died, and most were permanently sterilized. In 2002, Bill Gates forcibly vaccinated

South African children
against meningitis.
Many of these children
developed permanent
paralysis and the press
had called Bill Gates
`ruthless and immoral`.
In 2010, Gates gave his
anti-malaria vaccine to
5,000 African children.
151 of those children
died, 1000 had serious
side effects, paralysis
and seizures. Oh there`s
more. In 2014, the
World Health
Organization, funded by

Bill Gates, chemically sterilized millions of Kenyan women with Gates` tetanus vaccine, which the World Health Organization later admitted was poisonous.

Bill Gates has donated $10billion to the World Health Organization to help reduce the population through mass vaccinations. Almost everywhere you look

you will uncover bribe
money from Bill Gates.
He has bribed the CDC,
Anthony Fauci, Vaccine
impact modelling
consortium, Glaxo
Smith Kline, the
Pirbright Institute,
Merial Animal Health
Institute, Pfizer,
Harvard, Wellcome
trust, GAVI, CEPI,
UNICEF, WHO, DFID,
and Chris Witty. In a
speech, Italian
politician, Sara Cunial
called for the arrest of

Bill Gates for crimes against humanity. In her speech she stated that children will suffer and lose more from forced lockdowns and forced vaccinations. She referred to these children as `raped souls` for whom the right to schooling will only be granted with a bracelet (vaccine pass) which will get them used to slavery. She then made the following statement to Italian Prime Minister

Giuseppe Conte: "*The next time you receive a phone call from Bill Gates, forward it directly to the International Criminal Court for crimes against humanity*".

Bill Gates has funneled money into media outlets such as, BBC news, The Guardian, nutopia, The Seattle Times, abc News, Financial Times, npr public radio, allAfrica, El País, participant media, ITVS, European Journalism Centre, endemot, and AlJazeera, to push his covid narrative. He has also invested $1.7 billion in training programs for journalists. I suspect this is why the mainstream media is not covering the thousands upon thousands of severe adverse reactions from the covid vaccine.

Bill Gates has said he wants richer countries to start eating synthetic meat. In an interview with MIT Technology he said, *"I think all rich countries should move to 100% synthetic beef. You can get used to the taste difference, and eventually that green premium is modest enough that you can sort of change the behavior of people, or use regulation to totally shift the demand"*, to which he then criticized politics for getting in the way. It`s no surprise then that since 2018, Bill has bought a total of 269,000 acres of farmland. I wonder why. It makes me wonder if Bill ordered Joe Biden to pay famers not to grow any crops. And who got paid to intentionally destroy nineteen food distribution plants in the US in 2022 alone? Is a manufactured food crises another way to reduce the population?

This man claims to care so much about the environment and the health of us and our children, yet he flew numerous times on Jeffrey Epstein`s (The pedophile who trafficked minors from his pedophile island) infamous private jet known as the "Lolita Express". Not only that, but it was documented

that he frequented
Epstein`s pedophile
island, even after
Epstein was arrested
briefly for sex
trafficking.

The United Nations

On the 25th of April 1945, the United Nations came into being. It was founded and funded by the

Rockefeller Foundation. The UN headquarters are in New York. New York was chosen because it is an extraterritorial site, just like Vatican City, London city, and Washington DC. Extraterritorial means the UN is legally shielded from any national charges of high treason. The Rockefellers are still waging war on national sovereignty and their main goal is still, and always will be, a one world government. The Rockefellers` United Nations greatly support and actively promote the Great Reset.

Another goal of theirs is the eradication of Judeo-Christian culture, in order to then re-educate the population to accept the new world religion. The global stock market crash will act as a

catalyst but before that,
people need to be
brainwashed into
accepting communism
to the point that they
will "love their
servitude".

 After I visited the
United Nations website,
I noticed that the UN
has a `spiritual
foundation`. This
foundation is called the
Lucis Trust. I then
visited their website
and saw, quite plainly

and openly, that they
are a Luciferian
organization. In fact, if
you visit their website,
lucistrust.org you will
see for yourself who
they openly worship.
The Lucis Trust
influences the policies
of the UN, and it was
one of the first NGO`s
to be given consultative
status with the UN.

Every single one these
self-appointed elites are

evil to the core. They don't care about the people, and they would rather see us either dead or as slaves serving them. They are all connected to each other through their attempt at for global depopulation. Remember, "They`re all in this together".

The United Nations so called peacekeeping troops have faced numerous lawsuits over

the years. From
corruption and
lawlessness to
spreading deadly
diseases and even
sexually abusing
civilians of the countries
they occupy. It has been
documented around
the world and the UN
sparked anger by
claiming to be immune
as Haitians die from
cholera which has been
spread by its
peacekeepers. The first
lawsuit was filed in the

US courts as the UN`s soldiers were responsible for an outbreak of cholera in Haiti which has claimed the lives of 10,000 Haitians. In the Ivory Coast, the UN and the French government, with support from the Obama administration, back brutal Islamist militias to overthrow the Christian president of the country. They waged a brutal war and installed a Muslim banker as president in a campaign which left thousands of innocent Christians massacred in the country. In US documents, released by WikiLeaks, UN troops were exposed to be raping young Ivorian girls. Despite those, and numerous other atrocities, the UN continues to grow more powerful and is on the verge of transforming itself into a global government. At one point there was global uproar because several Uruguayan troops serving under the UN, held down and gang raped a teenage boy. The UN, however, were more concerned about the exposure which would tarnish their image.

In 2007, it was discovered that girls as young as thirteen were having sexual intercourse with UN "peacekeepers" for as little as $1 in Haiti. Sri Lankan soldiers were also accused of systematically raping Haitian girls as young as seven years old. All this has been well documented and has been going on for decades. In Tanzania, "peacekeepers" have impregnated girls as young as thirteen and eleven peacekeepers are facing paternity claims. Although the UN has `zero tolerance` for towards sexual violence, actions speak louder than words. Gang rape, child and baby rape, prostitution and sex trafficking rings, murder and theft have been happening for decades.

The UN`s future plans are a danger to us also. Agenda 21 is a plan developed by the UN`s department of Economic and Social Affairs, Division for

Sustainable Development. The plan calls for governments to take control of all lands and not allow any of the decision making in the hands of private property owners. It involves the educational system, the energy market, the transportation system, the governmental system, the health care system, food production, and more. The plan is to restrict your choices, limit your funds, narrow your freedoms, and take away your voice. One of the ways to achieve this is manufacture consensus. Another is to groom and train future candidates for local offices. Another is to sponsor non-governmental groups that go into schools and train children. Another is to offer federal and private grants and funding for city

programs that further
the agenda. Another is
to educate a new
generation of land use
planners to require New
Urbanism. Another is
to convert factories to
other uses, introduce
energy measures that
penalize manufacturing,
and set energy
consumption goals to
pre-1985 levels.
Another is to allow
unregulated
immigration in order to
lower standards of

living and drain local resources. I'm sure we can all see these things happening in our cities already.

The UN has decided that governments will have absolute authority over all the worlds resources and demands we reduce consumption (while they fly around the world in their private jets) and live in crowded surveillance cities under government control,

with no freedom or
private property.
Agenda 21 will mean:
Depopulation of rural
areas in favour of cities,
people will have fewer
children, or none at all,
ridding people of
private property and
limit consumption and
production via taxes
and fees, social justice
and economic equality,
limits on automobile
use and public
transport, phase out
and eventually limit air

travel. The UN says the agenda is voluntary, but every puppet government in the world is signing up for it. The agenda is primarily about climate change and environment, but it goes much deeper than this. The agenda is expressed with careful and planned wording. So, any politician and government official who says words like "green agenda" or

"sustainable
development" is
working to implement
Agenda 21. It is touted
as a solution to
everything from climate
change to extreme
poverty but in actuality,
it is a plan to empower
a global governing
body.

George Soros

George Soros was born on the 12th of August 1930 in Budepest, Hugary, to a Jewish family. Soros changed his name in 1944 and claimed he was a Christian to avoid being sent to the death camps. His father changed their name from Schwartz to Soros. He revealed that he aided the Nazis` in seizing property from

Jewish holocaust
victims and he had
described it as "the best
time of his life".
Allegedly, he reveled in
the chaos and agony
around him.

In 1945, Soros
moved to England and
attended the London
school of economics. He
would often stand at
Speakers` Corner and
lecture about the
positives of
internationalism
(globalism) in the

Esperanto language which his father taught him. Esperanto was to be an international language. A one world language.

George Soros is one of the 1% billionaire elites and has also financially backed his favorite politicians, Barack Obama and Hilary Clinton. He has financially backed a lot of the upheaval we have seen over the years, such as the BLM protests which destroyed business and entire communities. He is a huge advocate of open borders and plays a big part in the massive migration crisis from the Middle East to the West. There is a growing number of countries who want George prosecuted for his crimes.

George Soros, it has been discovered, is spending millions of dollars on district

attorney races in
American cities. There is
acquittal after acquittal,
even of those who are
proven guilty. They are
being released back into
society to wreak havoc
again and again. He
wants to disassemble
the police force and
drastically change the
justice system to his
liking. I suspect that
he's doing all of this to
turn America (and most
of Europe) into third
world squalor so the

masses will have to depend on their governments to "fix" the problem, to which the solution will be a new world order under the guise of "peace", which is run by a one world government.

Over the past couple of decades George has poured millions of dollars into organizations and schemes aimed at empowering a global government. The

Wikileaks e-mails
exposed George
funding the United
Nations scheme to
flood the US and
Europe with Muslim
"refugees", many of
them are trained
fighters. Soros
foundations have also
funded the violent Black
Lives Matter movement
with tens of millions of
dollars.

   In November of 2018,
Slovenian website
"Nova24TV", revealed

that immigrants were
spotted in Bosnia and
Herzegovina using
MasterCard debit cards.
The cards they were
using to withdraw
money from ATM`s had
no names on them, just
numbers. This report
was picked up by other
websites which stated:
*"Now the mystery has
been solved regarding
how so many poor
migrants have been
able to fund their illegal
journeys to Europe. The*

UN, EU and George Soros, in partnership with MasterCard, have spent millions of dollars providing migrants with prepaid debit cards, and European taxpayers have not been informed that their taxes are being spent on handouts to illegal immigrants". The United Nations Refugee Agency (UNHCR) has admitted to launching a scheme which provided aid to 10.5 million people across 94 countries in which recipients can assess money via cash machines.

During the 1980`s and 1990`s, Soros funded revolutions in several European nations, including Croatia, Czechoslovakia, and Yugoslavia. He funneled money into the opposition parties and independent media in these countries. During and after the

chaos in these
countries, he invested
in assets in each of
these countries. He
benefitted greatly from
their regime change. In
May 2014, in an
interview with CNN,
Soros stated that he
was responsible for
establishing a
foundation in the
Ukraine that ultimately
led to the overthrow of
their elected president,
and installed a
president handpicked

by the US State
Department, which at
the time was headed by
Hillary Clinton. The war
in Donbass resulted in
the deaths of 10,000
people and the
displacement of 1.4
million. Soros, again,
financially benefitted
from this chaos. His
prize in the Ukraine was
the state-owned energy
company, Naftogaz.
Soros then had his US
cronies advise Ukraine's

puppet government to privatize Naftogaz.

The refugee migrant crisis in 2015 is also Georges doing. He had donated money to two of his organizations who advocate for the settlement of third world Muslims into Europe. In 2015, a Sky News reporter had found, on a Greek island, "Migrant Handbooks". The handbooks were written in Arabic and had been given to refugees before coming to Europe. These handbooks were handed out by a group called "Welcome to the EU". This group is funded by Georges` Open Society Foundation. All of these activities do not surprise me in the slightest considering Soros` business partner was Sir James Goldsmith, a cousin of the Rothschild family.

The World Health Organization

The World Health Organization is an agency of the corrupt United Nations that is concerned with international public health. It is the highest authority on health in the world. It is financed by the UN and, vaccine-obsessed, Bill Gates.

The Bill and Melinda Gates Foundation has donated more than $2billion to the WHO since the 90`s. Bill Gates has so much authority in the World Health Organization that he has attended press conferences between 2007 and 2017, sitting next to the WHO director at the time, Margaret Chan. I`ve noticed that since 2020, every major news media has given him a

platform to dictate to
the world what we can
and can`t do regarding
our own health. He is
not a doctor, has no
medical training
whatsoever. He owns
half of the mainstream
media is pays the other
half to work for him.
Therefore, he is able to
silence the voices of
thousands of doctors
and scientists who do
not agree with his
views.

Back to the World Health Organization. They are now pushing the COVAX program to mass-vaccinate humanity. The COVAX slogan is "No one is safe until everyone is safe". This is illogical to me because it implies that even if you are vaccinated, you still aren`t safe. I have seen, from my own personal experiences that the Covid vaccine does not halt or even slow down transmission and it requires several boosters to maintain efficacy.

The WHO are working towards the expansions of their powers in the form of "The Intenational pandemic treaty", which is tied to a digital passport and digital identification. This treaty would aim to shift government authority to the WHO during any future pandemics.

(Considering the corruption within the WHO, there will be more pandemics). This treaty would allow the WHO to determine what constitutes a pandemic and what steps a country should take. Governments in these states will have no authority. Leslyn Lewis, member of the Canadian Parliament has warned *"we would end up with a one-size-fits-all approach for the entire world"*. She also cautioned that pandemics need not be limited to infectious diseases and could include, for example, an obesity crisis. Another part of this plan involves a contract with a German company to develop a global vaccine passport system. It will link every person on the planet to a digital ID or QR code. This system will be mandatory and universal. They also dictate about a woman`s right to an abortion, often repeating the slogan, "my body, my choice", but apparently that slogan is irrelevant when it comes to vaccines.

WHO director-General, Tedros Adhanom Ghebreyesus, was known as an international criminal before he was appointed WHO directorGeneral. He has been accused of genocidal violence and human rights violations while he was minister of Ethiopian FMOH (Foreign Ministry of Health). During his time in the Ethiopian government, Ethiopia has been affected by Cholera almost every year because of his incompetency and his refusal to declare an epidemic which caused the disease to spread across the country. When ISIS slit the throats of Ethiopian migrants in Libya, Tedros took a very long time to identify the victims as Ethiopians and he also refused to identify them individually to help the victims` families. Tedros says that he is proud of his role as TPLF Executive member and minister for Foreign Affairs, which makes him responsible for the

atrocities committed on
the Ethiopian people
and the ethnic cleansing
and genocide against
the Amharas. The
Amhara people
reported systematic
discrimination and
human rights abuses.
The government
withheld food and
fertilizer from the
Amhara villagers. They
have also been denied
emergency healthcare.
In addition to this, 2
million Amhara were

found to have
"disappeared". In the
1990`s, the Tedros TPLF
was listed as a terrorist
organization in the US.
One of the first things
Tedros did, after
securing his job in the
WHO, was nominate
Robert Mugabe as the
goodwill ambassador to
the WHO. Mugabe was
the man who ordered
the killings of 20,000
people in Zimbabwe
during the 1980`s. In a
sane world, Tedros

would be put on trial at the International Criminal Court for his crimes.

In 2009, during the so-called swine flu pandemic, the Bureau of Investigative Journalism discovered that the World Health Organization (connected to pharmaceutical companies) profited from the scare tactics they used to promote the swine flu vaccine.

Over $4 billion was
invested in the swine flu
vaccine but without a
pandemic there would
be no use for them.
They used fear and
propaganda to push the
vaccine on people, and
then the money was
made. A German
magazine called the
swine flu "pandemic" a
total sham as the World
Health Organization
told the world that up
to seven million people

would die without this
vaccine.

The Jesuits

In this section I`m going
to introduce you to
humanities true enemy
(if you didn`t already
know) the Jesuits. The
Jesuits are an ancient
cult who has infiltrated
the Roman Catholic
church a long time ago.
They are often referred
to as "Black Nobility" or

"Papal Bloodlines". The founder of the illuminati, Adam Weishaupt was a Jesuit. After he began to dabble in the occult, he started to believe that the God of the Bible was the evil one and that Satan was good. He became a satanist and a 33rd degree freemason. Through his alleged communications with Satan himself, he believed he was meant to help the Antichrist come to power. In 1776 he founded the Order of the Illuminati and he planned to infiltrate governments, secret societies, and religions in order to create a new world order, but he knew it would never happen in lifetime.

The Jesuit Order was suppressed and shut down by Pope Clement the 14th in 1773 but it was restored again in 1814 by Pope Pius the

7th.

Even the Rothschilds and the Rockefeller family answer to the Jesuits. Those families just supply the money. The Jesuits have killed many people over the years because they do not tolerate resistance. The Jesuits are led by the Superior General of the Jesuits, also known as the "Black Pope". Their main goal is world domination. The Pope that we see is called the white Pope, and above him, the grey pope, and at the very top of the hierarchy is the Black Pope. His name is Arturo Sosa.

The Jesuit oath of introduction is also known as the blood oath, or the 4th vow. It`s a brutal oath but it shows you just how violent they are. The oath is as follows: "*I furthermore promise and declare that I will, when opportunity*

*presents, make and
wage relentless war,
secretly or openly;
against all heretics,
protestants, and
liberals, as I am directed
to do so, to extirpate
and exterminate them
from the face of the
whole earth; and that I
will spare neither age,
sex, or condition; and
that I will hang, waste,
boil, flay, strangle and
busy alive these
heretics, rip up the
stomachs and wombs of*

*their women and crush
their infants` heads
against the walls, in
order to annihilate
forever their execrable
race. That when the
same cannot be done
openly, I will secretly
use the poisoned cup,
the strangling cord, the
steel of poniard or the
leaden bullet,
regardless of the honor,
rank, dignity, or
authority of the person
or persons, whatever
may be their condition*

in life, so either public or private, as I at any time may be directed to do so by any agent of the Pope or superior of the brotherhood of the holy faith, of the society of Jesus".

The Jesuits control every government as well as their leaders and they also control every intelligence agency in the world. The Rothschilds and Rockefellers are just their puppets, Jesuits agents operating under a Jewish front.

Back to Adam Weishsupt. His plan required the illuminati to do the following things in order to accomplish their purpose. They are as follows:

• Use money and sex bribery to obtain power and blackmail people who already

have high positions of
power.
- Grant scholarships to
those mentally gifted.
Indoctrinate them with
special training in
colleges to accept the
idea of the new world
order. ● Obtain control
of the press and any
other agency which
distributes
information. News and
information must be
tampered with so the
`goyim` would come to
believe that a world

one government is the only answer to our problems.

In 1784, a copy of the Sabbatean Frankist document was sent to Adam Weishaupt.

Ian Paisely, and Irish MP once said, *"The Jesuit is inwardly a devil, outwardly a monk and altogether a serpent"*. According to former Jesuit priest, Alberto Rivera, Jesuits regularly hold black

masses to worship
Satan. Being a former
Jesuit priest, he stated
that he attended these
masses and noticed
some high-level Jesuits
wearing Masonic
jewelry and rings.

Former Bishop
Gerard Bouffard of
Guatemala said that
Jesuits, through the
black pope, actually
control the Vatican
hierarchy and the
Roman Catholic Church.
Bouffard is now a born-

again Christian after working for six years in the Vatican. He stated, *"The man known as the black pope controls all major decisions made by the pope and he in turn controls the illuminati. I know this to be true since I worked for years for Pope John Paul 2nd. The Pope takes his marching orders from the Jesuit black pope as the Jesuits are the leaders of the new world order, with the task of infiltrating other religions and governments of the world in order to bring about a new world fascist government and a one world religion based on Satan and Lucifer"*. Researcher Bill Hughes confirmed this in his book "The Enemy Unmasked" and "The Secret Terrorists". Another researcher who confirmed this is Eric Jon Phelps, author of "Vatican Assassins".

Sabbatean Frankists

In 1666, Sabbatai Zevi declared himself the Messiah. He proclaimed that one could be redeemed through acts of sin. He had a large following of over one million people, half of the world's Jewish population. Sabbateans took part in and encouraged sexual promiscuity, incest, adultery, and religious orgies. He died in 1676 and a successor, named Jacob Frank, continued the occult philosophy. Frank claimed he was the reincarnation of their Messiah, Sabbatai Zevi. He performed strange and terrible acts, such as ritual sacrifice, eating fats forbidden by Jewish laws, and promoting orgies, sexual immorality, and he would sleep with his followers, as well as his own daughter. He preached about the ways in which to cross every boundary and mix the sacred with the profane.

He eventually formed an alliance with Adam Weishaupt and Meyer Amschel Rothschild, and they called their alliance the Order of the Illuminati. Their objective was was

to infiltrate world
religions and world
governments, to
destroy them from
within in an attempt to
bring about global
communism, which
would be ruled by
them, The New World
Order. Over the
centuries they have
managed to gain almost
total control of the
world`s media,
financiers, academic
leaders and politicians.
The Sabbateans believe

that sin is holy and should be practiced. They believed the Messiah would come when people either become righteous or corrupt, and they chose the latter.

Their grip on humanity is tight, that they can make a war against us look normal, and when we have figured out their plot, they convince everyone that it is racist to believe it. In the past,

Jacob Frank would be known to reverse the truth. He once said, "*Since we can`t all be saints, let us all be sinners. To ascend one must first descend. No man can climb a mountain until he has first descended to its roots. I did not come into this world to lift you up but rather to cast you down to the bottom of the abyss... The descent into the abyss requires not only* *the rejection of all religions, but also the commission of strange acts, and this in turn demands voluntary degradation of one`s own sense of self"*. It sounds to me, like the ravings of a lunatic with delusions of grandeur. He wrote the doctrine of the Antichrist, allegedly inspired by Satan, which permitted sexually promiscuous rites such as incest, rape and intercourse

with children. Another
one of Frank`s teachings
was to accumulate
wealth and riches even
by the most criminal
and devious actions. He
would, towards the end
of his life, nominate his
daughter Eva, or Eve, to
continue with the
movement, which she
did, until her death in
1816.

The CIA

This section will most likely be hard to read, considering the extent and the number of crimes committed by the CIA.

Project MK-Ultra was a CIA project to see how far they could take behaviour modification in people. It is the most well know story of mind control in history and if it wasn`t for someone requesting a freedom of information act regarding MK-Ultra, then we would never have heard about it at all.

It began in 1953 because American officials were allegedly concerned about their opponents (the Soviets). The CIA believed they could use psychedelic drugs, torture, and manipulation to destroy a person`s ego and

essentially scramble
their brain. Once this
was achieved, they
would repeat messages
and ideas to the subject
to build a new ego with
a purpose. These
experiments went on
for twenty years, from
1953 to 1973, and many
subjects didn`t even
know they were being
tested on. They used to
entice heroin addicts in
from the streets with
the promise of heroin
for participating.

Eventually they turned to more intense forms of mind control and torture after they decided that LSD was too unreliable.

Sidney Gottlieb bought the entire world`s supply of LSD for these experiments. He began distributing it in different places to see its effects. Some of his earliest experiments included dosing inmates and

college students to
see how it would
affect them. He also
dosed patients at
mental institutions.
These patients were
also unaware of the
experiments. In 1953,
Dr. Frank Olson, who
was an employee at
Fort Detrick, jumped
to his death from his
hotel room window in
New York City a week
after unknowingly
taking LSD while at a
meeting with the CIA.

The CIA were said to have hired torture specialists to help them carry out torture methods. It`s rumoured that one of these torture specialists was Josef Mengele. The experiments were not limited to America though, but also in Canada and Western Europe. The experiments in Europe consisted of criminals, who agreed

to the testing in
exchange for reduced
sentences. Testing
was also carried out
on the criminals who
refused. These tests
involved a variety of
torture methods, such
as, sleep deprivation,
electroshock, and
high doses of
psychedelic drugs.

The Canadian
"Driving experiments"
were carried out by
Donald Ewen Cameron,
which involved carrying

out tests in Canadian
prisons and psychiatric
hospitals. Subjects were
often placed into an
involuntary coma for
weeks or months at a
time. He would then
deliver repeated
messages to the
subjects while they
were unconscious to
plant ideas and fake
memories in their
heads. When the
subjects were given
very high doses of LSD,
Cameron would watch

them to see how they would cope with the hallucinations.

It has been said that the MK-Ultra mind control methods have not ended but simply been renamed under a different program. It has been widely reported that the US military and CIA torture American children as part of the mind-control experiments.

Retired NYPD detective, James

Rothstein, was tasked
with investigating a
child trafficking
operation. He
discovered that it went
all the way to the White
House. He found that
the child sex trafficking
operation was
coordinated by the CIA,
in collaboration with
the UK and Australian
secret services. He
found that it involved
blackmail where a child
prostitute was used to
trap and compromise

politicians, businessmen and high government officials.

Fiona Barnett, child trafficking victim, told her horrific story. She said, *"Under Kim Beazley`s administration, I was prostituted at six years old, to a paedophile orgy at parliament house in Canberra, where I was raped by then Prime Minister, Gough Whitlam, Lionel Murphy, and John Kerr.*

*Future Prime Minister
Bob Hawke raped me in
a suburban backyard
and Richard Nixon
raped me in the back of
a CIA military plane. I
was then raped by
media founder Ted
Turner on a trip to
Disneyland, and I was
trafficked to a summer
camp in Bohemian
Grove. At Bohemian
Grove I was one of a
group of children
dressed as teddy bears
and hunted for sport by*

men in the forest to the tune of teddy bears picnic".

Paul A. Bonacci said that as a child, he was kidnapped, tortured, subjected to sex abuse and mind control. In court he won $1,000,000 in damages and in his testimony, he said top members of the military and top politicians were involved in child abuse. He testified on videotape in 1990 and said that while he was on a trip, he was forced at gunpoint to commit homosexual acts on another boy, after which, the boy was shot in the head.

Nathalie Augustina for years was a highly sought-after model. She worked with major fashion brands such as Armani, Chanel and Dior. She revealed her story in her 2018 book,

"Nathalie- Confessions of a Top Model". In her book she revealed that she grew up an orphan and was placed in a paedophile foster family. They regularly took her, and many other children, to the government headquarters in The Hague. She stated that there were underground rooms where they were all raped. Along with other children, she was

subjected to mind
programming, where
some children were
programmed to enter
the fashion, film or
music industry, and
other children were
intended only for rape.
(The next few sentences
will shock you). Nathalie
returned to the
Netherlands because
she saw that a political
party which had been
approved by the
government, published
"Handbook on

Paedophilia". She was court-martialled by an organization called "Scientific Journalism for Paedophilia" which claims that sexual relations between young children and adults contribute to preparing the children as desired by the Dutch paaedophile state. This organization is funded by the Dutch government.

CIA officer, John
Kiriakou explains that
there are no moral
boundaries within the
CIA, there are no ethics,
and every law must be
broken in order to do a
spy job. He also said
that in exchange for
information or
cooperation, influential
people demand,
money, power, and
children.

"The fight to protect
our children is one we
must fight together"

www.ingramcontent.com/pod-product-compliance
Lightning Source LLC
Chambersburg PA
CBHW060046260726
48658CB00004B/1204